A. Harford Pearson

Burial offices according to the English and Roman uses

A. Harford Pearson

Burial offices according to the English and Roman uses

ISBN/EAN: 9783742836786

Manufactured in Europe, USA, Canada, Australia, Japa

Cover: Foto ©Andreas Hilbeck / pixelio.de

Manufactured and distributed by brebook publishing software
(www.brebook.com)

A. Harford Pearson

Burial offices according to the English and Roman uses

Burial Offices

ACCORDING TO THE

ENGLISH AND ROMAN USES.

EDITED BY

A. HARFORD PEARSON, Esq.,

(Barrister-at-Law),

TRANSLATOR OF THE "SARUM MISSAL IN ENGLISH," ETC.

———————

LONDON:

CHURCH PRINTING COMPANY,

11, BURLEIGH STREET, STRAND.

1880.

INTRODUCTION.

It is absolutely necessary, in dispassionately dealing with the subject of Christian burials, that we should divest ourselves of modern ideas as regards mourning and funerals, with which the Offices here printed have nothing in common.

The first question which naturally arises is, What is the meaning of the consecration of ORIGIN OF THE a Churchyard, and of the term "con-BLESSING OF secrated ground?" Fully to under-CHURCH- stand this, we must revert to the cir-YARDS. cumstances of early Christianity. It is a popular notion that Christianity—by which people generally mean the outward organization of the Churches which they see —sprang, like Minerva, complete into the world. They do not realise that primitive Christianity, in many of its outward forms, was very unlike the Christianity of the present day. The Roman or Greek, when he became a Christian, did not change his identity. A convert of those days Christianized the existing Pagan customs. To take an example : It had been a Pagan custom in Rome to knock a nail into a new house, by way of invoking the protection of some deity ; the Roman convert to Christianity continued to knock in the nail, only that upon it was inscribed our Lord's Name, or some Christian emblem. The hot cross buns on Good Friday are likewise a remnant of a heathen custom. The early Church, on the reception of a man, did not rudely sever him from existing customs, but contented herself with Chris-

B 2

tianizing them. The invocation of the blessing of tutelary deities upon articles in common use was one of those which she so utilised, and the hallowing or blessing of earth for purposes of interment is a very early form of it. As Sir G. Bowyer, in a recent letter to the *Times*, has pointed out, the term "consecration" of a Churchyard is a misnomer. The *blessing* of a Churchyard is, in its essence, the same as the blessing of food or holy water. We purposely add the latter because, whilst the Puritans strongly objected to its use, his descendant, the modern Dissenter, throwing over one of the prejudices for which his forefathers were tortured, exerts every influence at his command for the permission to be buried in "consecrated earth."

The chief characteristic of all Christian Burial Offices, Eastern and Western, con-
PRAYERS FOR sists in prayers for the dead. The
THE DEAD. mode in which these are worded, and the consequent doctrines involved, vary extremely, from the most spiritual to the most material. The basis of these Offices the translator believes to have been, like that of the Breviary, Judaic. This may, he thinks, be seen in the constant reiteration of the term "bosom of Abraham" as the place of the departed soul. There is, at all events, no doubt that prayers for the dead are Jewish in their origin, as can at once be seen in the inscriptions in the Jewish catacombs at Rome. Over the subject of prayers for the departed controversy has raged, possibly, more fiercely than over any other theological question. A large number of persons understand by prayer for the dead prayer that

one who has been condemned may attain to a place of peace. This is, of course, untrue. Prayer for the dead is founded on the reasonable belief that in the next world, as in this, we progress in goodness. Few thinking people can believe that we ourselves at once become perfect. Indeed, the most superficial idea of the perfect holiness of Almighty God, the approach to which is one great end of our creation, and of the proneness of our human nature to sin, makes it difficult to imagine that the greatest saint can at the moment of exit from this world be, in even a limited sense, perfect. In the natural order of things there are no leaps. The child becomes the man, the bad becomes worse, the good better, only by gradual progression; the habit of sin provokes sin, the habit of goodness engenders goodness. What these opposite principles are we know not; all we know of them is that they are progressive, and therefore the Jewish and Christian Churches have maintained the necessity of prayers for the dead, as well as prayers for the living. It is, however, easy to see how such a belief can be materialized. The traffickers for the sale of indulgences and the popular doctrine of purgatory in the middle ages, familiar to any who have studied the theological literature of those times, are examples of this. On the other hand, the purely material view taken, even now, by many Christians of eternal punishment, is an illustration of the same materialization outside the Roman Church. No restriction has ever been placed on these speculative opinions, and perhaps wisely; for as long as this world lasts the conditions existing in the intermediate state will be a subject of discussion. Meantime, the question is well summed up in the very mild definition of the Western Church in the Council of Trent :—" There is a purgatory, and the souls there detained are relieved by the suffrages of the faithful. . . . . The holy Synod enjoins on Bishops that they diligently strive that the sound doctrine touching purgatory, delivered by the holy Fathers and sacred Councils, be believed, held, taught, and everywhere proclaimed by the faithful of Christ. But let the more difficult and subtle questions, and those which tend not to edification, and from which, for the most part, there is no increase of piety, be excluded from popular discourses before the uneducated multitude. In like manner, such things as are uncertain, or which labour under an appearance of error, let them not allow to be made public and treated of. But those things which tend to a certain kind of curiosity or superstition, or which savour of filthy lucre, let them prohibit as scandals and stumbling-blocks of the faithful." It will be here observed that the only doctrine of purgatory which is *de fide* in the Roman Church is comprised in less than twenty words. As for the word itself, which, perhaps deservedly, is unpleasant to English ears, it is, on the highest Western authority, only another name for the intermediate state.

Another prominent characteristic of the Offices here printed is their total ignoring MOURNING. of the existence of any coffin. Even down to the beginning of the last. century coffins were never used for the middle or lower classes, but only for very rich or distinguished persons. In using them universally, as we do in the present day, one of the chief features of the Burial Offices loses its significance. "Earth to earth, ashes to ashes, dust to dust," has no meaning when possibly three coffins, and not the body alone, is committed to the grave. Mourning, as understood by undertakers, is an invention long posterior to even the latest of the Offices here reprinted; and, like many ecclesiastical deformations, is a direct importation from France, dating from the reign of Louis XIV. If Cromwell and whitewash are the *bête noire* of Ecclesiologists, Louis XIV. and his innovations are equally the *bête noire* of Liturgiologists. Nothing can be more opposed to the Christianity of sixteen centuries than the feathers, plumes, mutes, and black introduced at the end of the seventeenth. Let it then be clearly understood that it was the body, without the coffin, which was committed to the grave. The prevailing colour for funerals was red. Of course, it is not denied that black and purple paraphernalia are to be found in old Church inventories; but as a general rule, red was the colour used, as may be proved by the well-known fact that red was the colour used in Churches on such days as Ash Wednesday and Good Friday, both in the English and in the Continental Uses.

Christianity is, fortunately, stronger than custom, and so it comes to pass that the Christian world of the present day, irrespective of sects, is gradually reverting to simpler methods of burial, and to the abolition of the mourning trappings of Louis XIV.

To turn now to the Offices reprinted. The OFFICES FOR THE DEAD. Sacramentary of Leofric dates, at the latest, from the tenth century, and this may be considered the norm from which the English Uses sprang. These Offices were, of course, expanded as time went on. The latest edition of the Sarum Use testifies to the extent to which additions had gone. The Translator has given a prominent position to the York Use, because it appears to him that it strikes the balance between prolixity and brevity. He has, however, united to it the Prayer commencing "I commend" (see page 14), which is only found in the Sarum Use.

The more he has investigated the ancient Uses, the more he is persuaded that nothing is proved by the absence of a Rubric or Collect. Space was everything with the early printer. No one can realise the position of those who printed old manuscripts unless they admit the truth of the fundamental law that "omission" is not "prohibition." The difference between the York and the Sarum Burial Offices consists, roughly, in the addition of the 148th to 150th Psalms, and of various lengthy Collects in the Sarum Office.

With regard to the Roman Offices, which will now be habitually used by Roman Clergy in our graveyards, that for the burial of an adult is singularly meagre. On the other hand, few Offices can be more beautiful than that for the burial of a child. It is, however, curious that what we understand as a Burial Service—i.e., a Service at the grave—is in the Roman Offices only to be found in that for children.

We come now to our own Burial Office, which, as we have criticised other Offices, we are bound in fairness to criticise also. The first sentences consist of the Anthems used at the *Magnificat* and *Benedictus* of the old Offices, as well as part of the old Lessons. These are followed by two Psalms, with the selection of which no fault can be found, save that there was no apparent reason why the original ones should not have been retained. The chief defect of the Service appears to be the use of 1 Corinthians xv. as a Lesson. It is extremely long for the purpose, and appears in other respects not quite suitable. The only other criticism we have to make is with regard to the Collect for the committal of the body to the grave. When examined carefully, the words are unexceptionable, but they certainly *seem* to imply that the deceased will arise with the just, and therefore savour of "judgment before the time." The prayer might well terminate, as in the original : In the Name of the Father, and of the Son, and of the Holy Ghost. Amen.

The Translator cannot conclude his introduction without saying a few words as to the BURIALS ACT recent Burials Act. If a recent letter OF 1880. to the *Times* is to be trusted, it simply legislates in England for the burial of persons of different Creeds in a common ground, as has been hitherto done abroad. The blessing of the individual grave by the Priest might in all cases be substituted for that of the Bishop over the whole Churchyard, and thus one of the subjects of controversy would be withdrawn. However persons may resent the Act, the Anglican Clergy are placed in no worse position than those in France, where a Catholic Priest and a Protestant Minister may be found officiating side by side.

ALL SOULS' DAY, 1880.

The Burial Office

ACCORDING TO

THE USE OF YORK.

The Burial Office

ACCORDING TO

THE USE OF YORK.

❡ *When the body is taken to the Church shall be sung :—*

℣. Deliver me, O Lord, from eternal death in that dreadful day when the Heavens and earth shall be moved :

℟. When Thou shalt come to judge the world by fire.

℣. That day of wrath, the day of trouble and distress, that awful and exceeding bitter day.

❡ *When the body approaches the Church:—*

Ant.—May the Angels.

Miserere mei, Deus.   Psalm li.

Have mercy upon me, O God, after Thy great goodness : according to the multitude of Thy mercies do away mine offences.

Wash me thoroughly from my wickedness : and cleanse me from my sin.

For I acknowledge my faults : and my sin is ever before me.

Against Thee only have I sinned, and done this evil in Thy sight : that Thou mightest be justified in Thy saying, and clear when Thou art judged.

Behold, I was shapen in wickedness : and in sin hath my mother conceived me.

But lo, Thou requirest truth in the inward parts : and shalt make me to understand wisdom secretly.

Thou shalt purge me with hyssop, and I shall be clean : Thou shalt wash me, and I shall be whiter than snow.

Thou shalt make me hear of joy and gladness : that the bones which Thou hast broken may rejoice.

Turn Thy face from my sins : and put out all my misdeeds.

Make me a clean heart, O God : and renew a right spirit within me.

Cast me not away from Thy presence : and take not Thy holy Spirit from me.

O give me the comfort of Thy help again : and stablish me with Thy free Spirit.

Then shall I teach Thy ways unto the wicked : and sinners shall be converted unto Thee.

Deliver me from blood guiltiness, O God, Thou that art the God of my health : and my tongue shall sing of Thy righteousness.

Thou shalt open my lips, O Lord : and my mouth shall shew Thy praise.

For Thou desirest no sacrifice, else would I give it Thee : but Thou delightest not in burnt-offerings.

The sacrifice of God is a troubled spirit : a broken and contrite heart, O God, shalt Thou not despise.

O be favourable and gracious unto Sion : build Thou the walls of Jerusalem.

Then shalt Thou be pleased with the sacrifice of righteousness, with the burnt-offerings and oblations : then shall they offer young bullocks upon Thine altar.

Eternal rest grant them, O Lord : and let light perpetual shine upon them.

Ant.—May the Angels conduct thee to Paradise, and at thy coming may the martyrs receive thee into the holy City Jerusalem.

> Lord, have mercy.
> Christ, have mercy.
> Lord, have mercy.

℣. Eternal rest grant him (her), O Lord ;

℟. And let light perpetual shine upon him (her).

℣. I believe verily to see the goodness of the Lord,

℟. In the land of the living.

℣. From the gates of Hell

℟. Deliver his (her) soul, O Lord.

℣. The Lord be with you ;

℟. And with thy spirit.

5

Let us pray.

Almighty, everlasting God, Whom no one entreateth without hope of mercy, grant that the soul of Thy servant who died confessing Thy Name may be numbered with Thy Saints. Through.

O God, the Creator and Redeemer of all the faithful, forgive the sins of Thy servants and handmaidens, and grant them through our prayers that pardon and forgiveness for which they have ever yearned. Who.

¶ After the Office of the Dead and Mass let the Priest say:—

℟. Help him (her), O ye Saints of God : come to his (her) aid, O Angels of the Lord ; receiving and offering his (her) soul in the sight of the Most High Christ, Who called thee ; take thee unto Himself, and may His Angels conduct and place thee in the bosom of Abraham.

Lord, have mercy.
Christ, have mercy.
Lord, have mercy.

Our Father.

Let us pray.

Enter not into judgment with Thy servant, O Lord, for in Thy sight can no man living be justified. Judge him (her) not, therefore, O Lord, whom the prayers of the faithful commend unto Thee, but of Thy mercy let him (her) who, whilst alive, was signed in the Name of the Trinity, escape Thy just vengeance. Through.

¶ Then let the body be censed while the following is said:—

℟. Before I was born Thou knewest me ; in Thine own image didst Thou create me. I only give back my soul unto Thee, my Creator ; I am sorry for my offences, and am ashamed for that I have committed. When Thou comest to judge me, condemn me not.

Lord, have mercy.
Christ, have mercy.
Lord, have mercy.

Our Father.

Let us pray.

O God, unto Whom all things live, and in Whom our
bodies do not perish by death, but are changed, we humbly
pray Thee that Thou wouldest wash away from the soul
of Thy servant and pardon whatever sins through the
deceits of the devil and its own wickedness it hath con-
tracted; and that Thou wouldest lead it by the hands of
Thy Angels into the bosom of the Patriarchs Abraham,
Isaac, and Jacob, where it may escape all sorrow and
misery, so that in the last day it, together with the souls of
Thy faithful, may be made a partaker of Thy everlasting
glory, which eye hath not seen, nor ear heard, nor hath it
entered into the heart of man to conceive, but which
Thou hast prepared for them that love Thee.   Through.

¶ *Here let the body be censed.*

℣. Woe is me, O Lord, for I have sinned exceedingly
in my life.   Whither shall I flee but unto Thee, my God ?
Have mercy upon me when Thou comest in the last day.

℞. My soul is excessively disquieted, but do Thou, O
Lord, help it.

Lord, have mercy.
Christ, have mercy.
Lord, have mercy.

Our Father.

Let us pray.

Have mercy, we beseech Thee, O Lord, on this Thy
servant, that he (she) who desired to follow Thy will receive
not the consequences of his (her) sins ; but as here the true
faith united him (her) to the number of the just, so
there in Thy mercy Thou wouldest allow him (her) to be
numbered with the Angels.

Lord, have mercy.
Christ, have mercy.
Lord, have mercy.

¶ *Here let the Priest ask those present to pray for him.*

Our Father.

℣. Eternal rest grant them, O Lord ;

℟. And let light perpetual shine upon them.

℣. I believe verily to see the Lord in the land of the living.

℟. From the gates of Hell deliver their souls, O Lord.

℣. The Lord be with you ;

℟. And with thy spirit.

Let us pray.

For a Priest.

Almighty, everlasting God (see page 5).

For a Man.

Incline Thine ear, O Lord, to our prayers, we humbly beseech Thee ; and grant that the soul of Thy servant, whom Thou hast caused to depart from this world, may live in the place of light and peace, and may have a lot with Thy Saints.   Through.

For a Woman.

We beseech Thee, O Lord, in Thy pity have mercy on the soul of Thy servant, that she, being freed from contact with this mortal body, may have a part in life everlasting. Through.

¶ *Here let the body be sprinkled and censed thrice, and taken to the grave.*

Ant.—Open me.

Confitemini Domino.   Psalm cxviii.

O give thanks unto the Lord, for He is gracious : because His mercy endureth for ever.

Let Israel now confess, that He is gracious : and that His mercy endureth for ever.

Let the house of Aaron now confess : that His mercy endureth for ever.

Yea, let them now that fear the Lord confess : that His mercy endureth for ever.

I called upon the Lord in trouble : and the Lord heard me at large.

c

The Lord is on my side : I will not fear what man doeth unto me.

The Lord taketh my part with them that help me : therefore shall I see my desire upon mine enemies.

It is better to trust in the Lord : than to put any confidence in man.

It is better to trust in the Lord : than to put any confidence in princes.

All nations compassed me round about : but in the Name of the Lord will I destroy them.

They kept me in on every side, they kept me in, I say, on every side : but in the Name of the Lord will I destroy them.

They came about me like bees, and are extinct even as the fire among the thorns : for in the Name of the Lord I will destroy them.

Thou hast thrust sore at me, that I might fall : but the Lord was my help.

The Lord is my strength and my song : and is become my salvation.

The voice of joy and health is in the dwellings of the righteous : the right hand of the Lord bringeth mighty things to pass.

The right hand of the Lord hath the pre-eminence : the right hand of the Lord bringeth mighty things to pass.

I shall not die, but live : and declare the works of the Lord.

The Lord hath chastened and corrected me : but He hath not given me over unto death.

Open me the gates of righteousness : that I may go into them, and give thanks unto the Lord.

This is the gate of the Lord : the righteous shall enter into it.

I will thank Thee, for Thou hast heard me : and art become my salvation.

The same stone which the builders refused : is become the head-stone in the corner.

This is the Lord's doing : and it is marvellous in our eyes.

This is the day which the Lord hath made : we will rejoice and be glad in it.

Help me now, O Lord : O Lord, send us now prosperity.

Blessed be he that cometh in the Name of the Lord : we have wished you good luck, ye that are of the house of the Lord.

God is the Lord Who hath shewed us light : bind the sacrifice with cords, yea, even unto the horns of the altar.

Thou art my God and I will thank Thee : Thou art my God, and I will praise Thee.

O give thanks unto the Lord, for He is gracious : and His mercy endureth for ever.

Eternal rest grant them, O Lord : and let light perpetual shine upon them.

Ant.—Open me the gates of righteousness that I may go into them, and give thanks unto the Lord. This is the gate of the Lord, the righteous shall enter into it.

Our Father.

Let us pray.

Dearly beloved brethren, with the loving thoughts of devout remembrance let us remember the soul of our dear one whom the Lord hath taken away from the temptations of this world, beseeching our Lord God, in His mercy, that He would be pleased to give unto him (her) a peaceful and quiet dwelling, that He would forgive him (her) all that by dangerous boldness he (she) hath done amiss, and grant him (her) entire pardon ; that whatever in this world by his (her) own fault, or that of others, may have been his (her) transgressions, these, by His unspeakable loving-kindness and goodness, may be wholly blotted out and wiped away. Through.

Ant.—I will go.

Quemadmodum. Psalm xlii.

Like as the hart desireth the water-brooks : so longeth my soul after Thee, O God.

c 2

My soul is athirst for God, yea, even for the living God : when shall I come to appear before the presence of God ?

My tears have been my meat day and night : while they daily say unto me, Where is now thy God ?

Now when I think thereupon, I pour out my heart by myself : for I went with the multitude, and brought them forth into the house of God ;

In the voice of praise and thanksgiving : among such as keep holy day.

Why art thou so full of heaviness, O my soul : and why art thou so disquieted within me ?

Put thy trust in God : for I will yet give Him thanks for the help of His countenance.

My God, my soul is vexed within me : therefore will I remember Thee concerning the land of Jordan, and the little hill of Hermon.

One deep calleth another, because of the noise of the water-pipes : all Thy waves and storms are gone over me.

The Lord hath granted His loving-kindness in the day-time : and in the night season did I sing of Him, and made my prayer unto the God of my life.

I will say unto the God of my strength, Why hast Thou forgotten me : why go I thus heavily, while the enemy oppresseth me ?

My bones are smitten asunder as with a sword : while mine enemies that trouble me cast me in the teeth ;

Namely, while they say daily unto me : Where is now thy God ?

Why art thou so vexed, O my soul : and why art thou so disquieted within me ?

O put thy trust in God : for I will yet thank Him, which is the help of my countenance, and my God.

Eternal rest grant them, O Lord : and let light perpetual shine upon them.

Ant.—I will go into the Tabernacle, even into the house of God.

> Lord, have mercy.
> Christ, have mercy.
> Lord, have mercy.

11

Let us pray.

Almighty, everlasting God, we humbly entreat Thy mercy that as Thou hast created man in Thine image, Thou wouldest graciously receive the soul of Thy servant, whom Thou hast this day commanded to depart hence, and hast taken to Thyself. Let not the shadow of death or the blackness of darkness overcome him (her), but pardon all his (her) offences, that he (she) may attain unto a place of refreshment and peace in the bosom of the Patriarch Abraham, so that when the Day of Judgment arrives he (she) may arise again with Thy Saints. Through.

¶ Here let the body be sprinkled with holy water, and censed, and placed in the grave, the Priest first saying :—

We humbly pray Thee, O Lord Almighty, everlasting God, to bl✠ess and sanc✠tify this grave and the body we place in it, that he (she) who lieth in it may obtain the salvation of his (her) soul, and be protected from the assaults of the enemy. Through.

Ant.—This shall be.

Memento, Domine. Psalm cxxxii.

Lord, remember David : and all his trouble ;

How he sware unto the Lord : and vowed a vow unto the Almighty God of Jacob ;

I will not come within the tabernacle of mine house : nor climb up into my bed ;

I will not suffer mine eyes to sleep, nor mine eye-lids to slumber : neither the temples of my head to take any rest ;

Until I find out a place for the temple of the Lord : an habitation for the mighty God of Jacob.

Lo, we heard of the same at Ephrata : and found it in the wood.

We will go into His tabernacle : and fall low on our knees before His foot-stool.

Arise, O Lord, into Thy resting-place : Thou, and the ark of Thy strength.

Let Thy priests be clothed with righteousness : and let Thy saints sing with joyfulness.

For Thy servant David's sake : turn not away the presence of Thine Anointed.

The Lord hath made a faithful oath unto David : and He shall not shrink from it.

Of the fruit of thy body : shall I set upon thy seat.

If thy children will keep My covenant, and My testimonies that I shall learn them : their children also shall sit upon thy seat for evermore.

For the Lord hath chosen Sion to be an habitation for Himself : He hath longed for her.

This shall be my rest for ever : here will I dwell, for I have a delight therein.

I will bless her victuals with increase : and will satisfy her poor with bread.

I will deck her priests with health : and her saints shall rejoice and sing.

There shall I make the horn of David to flourish : I have ordained a lantern for Mine Anointed.

As for his enemies, I shall clothe them with shame : but upon himself shall his crown flourish.

Eternal rest grant them, O Lord : and let light perpetual shine upon them.

Ant.—This shall be my rest for ever ; here will I dwell, for I have a delight therein.

> Lord, have mercy.
> > Christ, have mercy.
> Lord, have mercy.
> Our Father.

Let us pray.

O God, with Whom do live the souls of the departed, and in Whom they enjoy perfect happiness after that they have put off the burden of the flesh, grant, we beseech Thee, that the soul of Thy servant, who in this life lacked the light of Thy countenance, may enjoy it for ever. Let no torment of death touch him (her) or fear assail him (her) ;

number him (her) not amongst the wicked, but grant him (her) pardon of his (her) offences, and the enjoyment of the peace he (she) desireth. Through.

¶ The Absolution over, the body in the grave.

The Lord Jesus Christ, Who hast given to His Apostle S. Peter and the rest of His Disciples the power of binding and loosing, deliver thee from the chains of thy sins ; and in so far as it is permitted to my frailty, I absolve thee before the Judgment Seat of our Lord Jesus Christ, and mayest thou have life eternal for ever. Amen.

¶ Here let the body be sprinkled with holy water, and censed, and let earth be placed on the body in the form of a cross.

Ant.—Of earth.

Domine probasti. Psalm cxxxix.

O Lord, Thou hast searched me out, and known me : Thou knowest my down-sitting and mine up-rising ; Thou understandest my thoughts long before.

Thou art about my path, and about my bed : and spiest out all my ways.

For lo, there is not a word in my tongue : but Thou, O Lord, knowest it altogether.

Thou hast fashioned me behind and before : and laid Thine hand upon me.

Such knowledge is too wonderful and excellent for me : I cannot attain unto it.

Whither shall I go then from Thy Spirit : or whither shall I go then from Thy presence ?

If I climb up into Heaven, Thou art there : if I go down to Hell, Thou art there also.

If I take the wings of the morning : and remain in the uttermost parts of the sea ;

Even there also shall Thy hand lead me : and Thy right hand shall hold me.

If I say, Peradventure the darkness shall cover me : then shall my night be turned to day.

Yea, the darkness is no darkness with Thee, but the night is as clear as the day : the darkness and light to Thee are both alike.

For my reins are Thine : Thou hast covered me in my mother's womb.

I will give thanks unto Thee, for I am fearfully and wonderfully made : marvellous are Thy works, and that my soul knoweth right well.

My bones are not hid from Thee : though I be made secretly, and fashioned beneath in the earth.

Thine eyes did see my substance, yet being imperfect : and in Thy book were all my members written.

Which day by day were fashioned : when as yet there was none of them.

How dear are Thy counsels unto me, O God : O how great is the sum of them !

If I tell them they are more in number than the sand : when I wake up I am present with Thee.

Wilt Thou not slay the wicked, O God : depart from me, ye blood-thirsty men.

For they speak unrighteously against Thee : and Thine enemies take Thy Name in vain.

Do not I hate them, O Lord, that hate Thee : and am not I grieved with those that rise up against Thee ?

Yea, I hate them right sore : even as though they were mine enemies.

Try me, O God, and seek the ground of my heart : prove me, and examine my thoughts.

Look well if there be any way of wickedness in me : and lead me in the way everlasting.

Eternal rest grant them, O Lord : and let light perpetual shine upon them.

Ant.—Of earth hast Thou formed me, and clothed me in the flesh, O Lord : renew me in the last day.

¶ *Here shall the Priest say :—*

I commend thy soul to God the Father Almighty. Earth to earth, ashes to ashes, dust to dust ; in the Name of the Father, and of the Son, and of the Holy Ghost. Amen.

Lord have mercy.
Christ have mercy.
Lord have mercy.
Our Father.

Let us pray.

Let us pray, dearly beloved brethren, to God for the soul of our dear one, whom He hath pleased to deliver from the prison of this world, and whose body we this day commit to the grave, that He, in answer to our prayers, will place him (her) amongst His Saints and elect—Abraham, Isaac, and Jacob—that he (she) may have a part in the Resurrection that is to come.

Let us pray.

O God, Who deignest to listen to our prayers, and art ever with us, give Thy servant, whose funeral office we have this day performed, a place of reward with Thy Saints and faithful. Through.

Let us pray.

O God, the Giver of life and Renewer of the body, Who willest to be petitioned by sinners, hear the prayers which we pour forth with tears on behalf of the soul of Thy servant. Deliver him (her) from the pains of Hell, place him (her) with Thy Saints, and, clothing him (her) with a heavenly garment, do Thou place him (her) in the joys of Paradise. Through.

Let us pray.

O God, the eternal Lover of souls, deliver the soul of Thy servant from all pain, so that, inasmuch as he (her) whilst in the flesh had true faith, he (she) may be delivered from the pains of Hell, and, escaping them, may participate in the joys of the Saints. Through.

Awful is it, O Lord, that man should presume to commit man, he that is mortal mortality, and he that is dust dust, to Thee our Lord God ; yet forasmuch as earth receiveth earth, and dust is turned to dust, until all flesh is reduced into its original state, therefore do we, O God, most Holy Father, entreat Thee with tears that of Thy mercy Thou wouldest place the soul of Thy servant, whom Thou hast taken from the mire of this world, in the bosom of Abraham. Preserve him (her) from the flames of Hell, and give him (her) rest. Graciously pardon his (her) sins ; let him (her) not receive the consequences of sin, but have mercy on him (her), so that when this world is over he (she) may arise to be crowned together with Thy faithful on Thy right hand. Through.

Let us pray.

We who have buried that which is mortal humbly pray Thee, O God, unto Whom all live, that the body of our dear one which is buried in weakness may arise with Thy Saints, and that his (her) soul may be numbered with the faithful, and enjoy eternal glory and happiness. Through.

¶ *Here let the Priest bid prayers for him and all that rest in the Churchyard, and say :—*

De Profundis. Psalm cxxx.

Out of the deep have I called unto Thee, O Lord : Lord, hear my voice.

O let Thine ears consider well : the voice of my complaint.

If Thou, Lord, wilt be extreme to mark what is done amiss : O Lord, who may abide it ?

For there is mercy with Thee : therefore shalt Thou be feared.

I look for the Lord ; my soul doth wait for Him : in His word is my trust.

My soul fleeth unto the Lord : before the morning watch, I say, before the morning watch.

O Israel, trust in the Lord, for with the Lord there is mercy : and with Him is plenteous redemption.

And He shall redeem Israel : from all his sins.

Eternal rest grant them, O Lord : and let light perpetual shine upon them.

Lord, have mercy.
Christ, have mercy.
Lord, have mercy.

Our Father.

℣. Eternal rest grant them, O Lord ;

℞. And let light perpetual shine upon them.

℣. I believe verily to see God

℞. In the land of the living.

℣. From the gates of Hell

℞. Deliver our souls, O Lord.

℣. The Lord be with you ;

℞. And with thy spirit.

Let us pray.

May he (she) obtain a portion of the blessed Resurrection, and be worthy of eternal life in Heaven ; through Thee, O Jesus Christ, Saviour of the world, who.

Let us pray.

Absolve, we beseech Thee, O Lord, the soul of Thy servant from the chain of sin, that in the glorious Resurrection he (she) may rise again and live amongst Thy Saints and elect. Through.

Let us pray.

O God, in Whom the souls of the faithful have rest, grant unto Thy servants and handmaidens here and everywhere resting in Christ pardon of all their faults, that, being freed from their sins, they may be for ever happy with Thee. Through.

Let us pray.

O God, the Creator and Redeemer of all the faithful, forgive the sins of Thy servants and handmaidens, and grant them through our prayers that pardon and forgiveness for which they have ever yearned. Who.

May his (her) soul and the souls of all the faithful departed through the mercy of God rest in peace. Amen.

The Burial Office

ACCORDING TO

THE USE OF SARUM.

The Burial Office

THE USE OF SARUM.

¶ *The Office is the same as that of York until the body is taken to the grave, when is said:—*

Ant.—May the Angels (see page 3).

Psalm cxiv. and Psalm xxv., if necessary.

¶ *After which the Antiphon,* May the Angels, *is repeated.*

The Collect.

Dearly beloved brethren (see page 9).

We humbly entreat Thee, O Lord, holy Father, Almighty, everlasting God, on behalf of the soul of our brother (sister), whom Thou hast been pleased to call out of this world ; that Thou wouldest give him (her) the place of refreshment and peace. Let him (her) pass through the gates of Hell and the pains of darkness, and rest in the home of the Saints, and in the holy light which of old Thou promisedst to Abraham and his seed. Let not his (her) soul sustain hurt, but when the great day of Resurrection shall come, raise him (her) together with Thy Saints and elect, and utterly wipe out all his (her) sins, that he (she) may be partaker of Thy immortality with Thee. Through.

¶ *The Collects ended, let the grave be opened, and let the Anthem be sung :—*

Ant.—Open me (see page 7).

Psalm cxviii.

The Collect.

Almighty, everlasting God (see page 11).

O God, Who deignest (see page 15).

¶ Then let the grave be blessed.

We humbly pray Thee (see page 11).

Or the following may be used.

℣. Our help is in the Name of the Lord,

℟. Who hath made Heaven and earth.

Bless, O Lord, this grave, as Thou didst bless the graves of Abraham, Isaac, and Jacob.

℣. Shew us Thy mercy, O Lord ;

℟. And grant us Thy salvation.

The Collect.

O God, Who hast formed the earth and framed the heavens, and through baptism didst restore man when taken in the snares of death ; Who didst also bless and put in the Book of Life the Patriarchs Abraham, Isaac, and Jacob, after that they were dead ; Who raised our Lord Jesus Christ when He had overcome Hell, and wilt quicken the bodies of those that believe in Him ; vouchsafe, we beseech Thee, to bl✠ess this Thy servant (handmaiden), that he (she) may have rest in the bosom of Abraham. Who.

Regard, we beseech Thee, O Lord, this grave, and pour forth Thy Holy Spirit, that he (she) may rest in peace, and in the Day of Judgment may rise again with all Thy Saints. Who.

¶ Here let holy water be sprinkled on the grave, and let it be censed. Then shall be sung :—

Ant.—I will go (see page 9).

Psalm xlii.

¶ Which said, let the Priest say :—

Let us pray, dearly beloved (see page 15).

O God, the eternal Lover of souls (see page 15).

¶ *The Collects ended, let the grave be covered with the pall, the Priest saying:—*

The Lord Jesus Christ (see page 13).

¶ *Here let the grave be sprinkled with holy water, and censed.*

This shall be (see page 12).

Psalm cxxxii.

O God, with Whom (see page 12).

O Lord, Almighty God, incline Thine ear unto our prayers ; help and succour us, and receive the soul of Thy servant, that hath escaped from the chains of the body, into the peace of Thy Saints ; that being delivered from the place of pain, and fire of Hell, he (she) may be brought into the land of the living.   Through.

¶ *The Collects ended, let the officiant place earth on the body in the form of a Cross, and cense it, and sprinkle it with holy water ; and whilst the following Psalm is said, let the body be entirely covered with earth:—*

Ant.—Of earth (see page 13).

Psalm cxxxix.

I commend (see page 14).

Awful is it (see page 15).

O God, the Giver (see page 15).

Ant.—Let everything that hath breath praise the Lord.

Psalm cxlviii.—l. (see pages 40 and 41).

We who have buried (see page 16).   .

Ant.—I am the Resurrection.

Blessed be the Lord God.

℣. and ℟. as on page 36.

The Collect.

O God, the Source of pity, Father of mercies, the Comforter of those in sorrow, Who forgivest sin, and from Whom all goodness comes, graciously hear our prayers; and although our conscience is witness that we are unworthy to be heard, since Thou hast commanded sinners to pray to Thee, mercifully incline Thine ear to us who pray. Therefore, O Lord, holy Father, Almighty, everlasting God, we pray Thee that for the sake of Thy only Son Jesus Christ, Who wast incarnate of a Virgin, and Who by His atonement for sin through His blood gave life unto the world; absolve the soul of our brother (sister) whom Thou hast just delivered from the chains of this sinful body; and because Thou didst send Thy Son our Lord Jesus Christ to earth, let not his (her) soul suffer from the snares of the wicked; deliver it from the awful pains of Hell, that it know naught of darkness; but escaping from Thy just vengeance, suffer it to enjoy the blessing of eternal rest and happiness. Through.

To Thee, O Lord, we commit the soul of Thy servant, that, though dead, he (she) may live unto Thee; and do Thou mercifully wipe away whatever sins he (she) hath committed in his (her) conversation here on earth.

Ant.—Eternal rest.

Psalm li. (see page 3).

In behalf of the soul of ——, and of all those whose bodies lie here or elsewhere, let us say—

Our Father, and ℣. (see pages 6 and 7).

O God, in Whom the souls (see page 17).

¶ *Returning from the grave, let them say the seven Penitential Psalms, or :—*

Ant.—Eternal rest.

Psalm cxxx. (see page 16).

Lord, have mercy, &c.

Let us pray.

May the prayers of the holy Mother of God, Mary ever Virgin, of Thy Apostle St. Peter, and all Saints, as well as those of this Thy family, avail in behalf of the soul of our brother (sister) ; that he (she) may obtain forgiveness, and that he (she) whom Thou didst redeem through the precious blood of Thy Son our Lord Jesus Christ, may escape the pains of Hell. Through.

In a low voice.

May his (her) soul, and the souls of all the faithful departed, through the mercy of God rest in peace. Amen.

The Burial Office

ACCORDING TO

THE SACRAMENTARY OF LEOFRIC.

The Burial Office

ACCORDING TO

THE SACRAMENTARY OF LEOFRIC.

¶ *When the body is taken to the Church, let them sing:—*

Psalm li., and Versicles (see pages 3 and 4).

Receive, O Lord, the soul of Thy servant into Thy blessed habitation, and give it peace in the heavenly Jerusalem, that it may await the day of Resurrection in the bosom of Abraham, and, together with the blessed, may rise again at Thy right hand, and obtain everlasting life. Through.

O God, the eternal Lover (see page 15).

¶ *Let the body remain in the Church until Mass has been offered for it; after which, let the Priest stand next the bier, and say:—*

We humbly pray Thee, Almighty God, in Whom we live and die, that Thou wouldest grant eternal rest and peace unto the soul of our brother (sister), whom Thou hast taken from this world, in the bosom of Abraham, Isaac, and Jacob. Through.

℞. Help him (her) (see page 5).

O Lord God, Judge of all things, the God of Heaven, Earth, and Hell, we humbly pray Thee that Thou wouldest give peace unto the soul of our dear one, and a part in the first Resurrection. Through.

℣. Woe is me (see page 6).

O God, the Creator and Redeemer of all, Who art the joy of Thy Saints, do Thou for our prayers have mercy on the soul of our brother (sister), whom Thou hast released from the chains of his (her) body.   Through.

¶ *Let the body be then taken from the Church to the grave, and let the Priest say:—*

Ant.—Open me (see page 7).

Psalm cxviii.

Let us pray.

We humbly entreat Thee (see page 21).

Ant.—I will go (see page 9).

Psalm xlii.

We, who are overcome by sudden grief and soreness of heart, humbly implore Thee, the Fountain of pity, that in Thy mercy and loving kindness Thou wouldest receive the soul of our dear one who returneth unto Thee, and of Thy goodness wouldest mercifully wipe out whatever sins he (she) hath committed in the flesh, that he (she) may give thanks unto Thee ; and when he (she) is again united to the body, may be numbered with Thy Saints. Who.

¶ *Let the body be placed in the grave.*

Ant.—This shall be (see page 11).

Psalm cxxxii.

Let us pray, dearly beloved (see page 15).

Ant.—Of earth (see page 13).

Psalm cxxxix.

O Lord, Almighty, everlasting God, Who in Thy mercy permitteth us, who are not sufficient for ourselves, yet to pray for others ; receive the soul of Thy servant who returneth unto Thee, and let Michael, the Archangel of the Testament, be near him (her).   Deliver him (her) from the powers of darkness and the place of punishment, that he (she) be not overwhelmed with sin, but may be accepted by Thee, and have a place of refreshment in the bosom of Abraham, Isaac, and Jacob. Through.

We who have buried (see page 16).

Almighty, everlasting God, Who wast pleased to breathe the soul into the body of man, now that at Thy will dust is again turned unto dust, do Thou unite this Thine image unto the Saints and elect for ever. Through.

O God, with Whom (see page 12).

Almighty, everlasting God (see page 11).

O God, the only Physician after death, grant, we beseech Thee, that the soul of Thy servant, which hath been set free from all earthly contagion, may have a part in Thy redemption. Through.

O God, unto Whom (see page 6).

Awful is it (see page 15).

¶ *Then shall the Priest ask those present to pray.*

Our Father.

Versicles (see page 7).

May he (she) (see page 17).

Psalm li. (see page 3).

Absolve (see page 17).

The Commendation of the Soul.

We commend to Thee, O Lord, the soul of Thy servant, that he (she), though dead, may live unto Thee for ever, and that Thou wouldest, of Thy infinite mercy, wipe away and pardon the sins which he (she) hath of his (her) frailty committed in this world. Through.

We, who cannot of ourselves make satisfaction for sin, yet entreat Thy mercy, O Lord, Holy Father, Almighty, everlasting God, on behalf of others ; beseeching Thee that in Thy goodness Thou wouldest receive the soul of Thy servant, who returneth unto Thee; that Michael, the Angel of Thy Testament, be with him (her), and that Thou wouldest place him (her) by the hands of Thy Saints amongst Thy elect, in the bosom of the Patriarchs Abraham, Isaac, and Jacob; that he (she) being delivered from the shadow of darkness and the place of torment, be no longer overwhelmed by the sins that he (she) hath through ignorance or frailty committed, but be numbered with Thine elect and enjoy Thy blessed rest, so that in the day of Thy awful judgment he (she) may, together with Thy Saints, have for ever the fruition of Thy countenance. Through.

We commit the soul of Thy servant unto Thee, O Lord, beseeching Thee that forasmuch as in Thy mercy Thou didst come down to earth, Thou wouldest not withhold from him (her) a place in the bosom of the Patriarchs. Who.

The Burial Office

THE USE OF ROME.

The Burial Office

THE USE OF ROME.

¶ *Before the body is moved, let the Parish Priest sprinkle it with holy water, and say :—*

Ant.—If Thou, O Lord.

De profundis. Psalm cxxx.

(See page 16.)

Ant.—If Thou, O Lord, wilt be extreme to mark what is done amiss : O Lord, who may abide it ?

¶ *Then let the body be carried from the house and the Parish Priest intone :—*

Ant.—The bones which Thou hast broken.

Miserere mei, Deus. Psalm li.

(See page 3.)

Ant.—The bones which Thou hast broken shall rejoice.

¶ *According to the length of way other Psalms can be said, with the ending* Eternal rest, *instead of* Glory be.

¶ *On entering the Church shall be repeated the Anthem,* The bones which Thou hast broken, *and then*—

℞. Help him (her) (see page 5).

¶ *The bier being placed in the Church, let the Office of the Dead be said, and afterwards Mass. Mass ended, let the Priest say,* Enter not (*see page 5*). *Then let the Priest cense the body and say*—

℣. Deliver me, O Lord (see page 3).

Lord, have mercy.

Christ, have mercy.

Lord, have mercy.

℣. Deliver his (her) soul, O Lord,

℟. From the gates of Hell.

℣. May his (her) soul rest in peace.

℟. Amen.

℣. O Lord, hear our prayer ;

℟. And let our cry come unto Thee.

℣. The Lord be with you ;

℟. And with thy spirit.

Let us pray.

O God, Whose province is ever to pardon and have mercy, we humbly entreat Thee, on behalf of the soul of Thy servant, whom Thou hast this day called to depart hence, deliver it not over to the enemy, but receive it at the hands of Thy Angels into Paradise, that inasmuch as it believed in Thee, it suffer not the pains of Hell, but enjoy everlasting life. Through.

¶ *This Prayer ended, let the body be carried to the grave, the Clergy saying :—*

Help him (her) (see page 5).

¶ *When the grave is reached, if it be not blessed, let the Priest say :—*

Let us pray.

O God, in Whose mercy do rest the souls of the faithful, vouchsafe to bless this grave and give Thine Angels charge over it ; and deliver from the chains of all their sins the souls of all those whose bodies are buried here, that they may rejoice with Thy Saints. Through.

¶ *Which said, let the Priest sprinkle the grave with holy water, and cense the body and grave, and say :—*

Ant.—I am the Resurrection and the Life.

Benedictus. S. Luke i. 68

Blessed be the Lord God of Israel : for He hath visited, and redeemed His people ;

And hath raised up a mighty salvation for us : in the house of His servant David ;

As He spake by the mouth of His holy Prophets : which have been since the world began ;

That we should be saved from our enemies : and from the hands of all that hate us ;

To perform the mercy promised to our forefathers : and to remember His holy Covenant ;

To perform the oath which He sware to our forefather Abraham : that He would give us ;

That we being delivered out of the hand of our enemies : might serve Him without fear ;

In holiness and righteousness before Him : all the days of our life.

And Thou, Child, shalt be called the Prophet of the Highest : for Thou shalt go before the face of the Lord to prepare His ways ;

To give knowledge of salvation unto His people : for the remission of their sins,

Through the tender mercy of our God : whereby the day-spring from on high hath visited us ;

To give light to them that sit in darkness, and in the shadow of death : and to guide our feet into the way of peace.

Eternal rest grant them, O Lord : and let light perpetual shine upon them.

Ant.—I am the Resurrection and the Life : he that believeth in Me, though he were dead, yet shall he live : and whosoever liveth and believeth in Me shall never die.

Lord, have mercy.
Christ, have mercy.
Lord, have mercy.
Our Father.

¶ *Here let him sprinkle the corpse with holy water.*

℣. From the gates of Hell

℟. Deliver his (her) soul, O Lord.

℣. May he (she) rest in peace.

℟. Amen.

℣. O Lord, hear our prayers ;

℟. And let our cry come unto Thee.

℣. The Lord be with you ;

℟. And with thy spirit.

Let us pray.

Have mercy, we beseech Thee, O Lord, on this Thy servant, that he (she) who desired to keep Thy will receive not the consequences of his (her) sins, that like as the true faith hath united him (her) here unto the faithful, so there Thou wouldest number him (her) with Thy Angels. Through.

¶ *Then let the Priest say returning from the grave :—*

Ant.—If Thou, O Lord, wilt be extreme.

De profundis. Psalm cxxx.

(See page 16.)

Ant.—If Thou, O Lord, wilt be extreme to mark what is done amiss : O Lord, who may abide it ?

THE BURIAL OFFICE FOR CHILDREN.

¶ *When a child is dead, let him (her) be covered with flowers, and let the Priest, in surplice and white stole, sprinkle the body, and say :—*

Ant.—The Lord's Name is praised.

Laudate, pueri. Psalm cxiii.

Praise the Lord, ye servants : O praise the Name of the Lord.

Blessed be the Name of the Lord : from this time forth for evermore.

The Lord's Name is praised : from the rising up of the sun unto the going down of the same.

The Lord is high above all heathen : and His glory above the heavens.

Who is like unto the Lord our God, that hath His dwelling so high : and yet humbleth Himself to behold the things that are in Heaven and earth ?

He taketh up the simple out of the dust : and lifteth the poor out of the mire.

That He may set him with the princes : even with the princes of His people.

He maketh the barren woman to keep house : and to be a joyful mother of children.

Glory be to the Father, and to the Son : and to the Holy Ghost:

As it was in the beginning, is now, and ever shall be : world without end. Amen.

Ant.—The Lord's Name is praised from the rising up of the sun unto the going down of the same.

¶ *Whilst the body is carried to the grave, let the first part of* Psalm cxix. *and, if there is time,* Psalm cxviii. *be said. When they arrive at the Church, let the Priest say :—*

Ant.—He shall receive.

Domini est terra. Psalm xxiv.

The earth is the Lord's, and all that therein is : the compass of the world, and they that dwell therein.

For He hath founded it upon the seas : and prepared it upon the floods.

Who shall ascend into the hill of the Lord : or who shall rise up in His holy place ?

Even he that hath clean hands, and a pure heart : and that hath not lift up his mind unto vanity, nor sworn to deceive his neighbour.

He shall receive the blessing from the Lord : and righteousness from the God of his salvation.

This is the generation of them that seek Him : even of them that seek thy face, O Jacob.

Lift up your heads, O ye gates, and be ye lift up, ye everlasting doors : and the King of glory shall come in.

Who is the King of glory : it is the Lord strong and mighty, even the Lord mighty in battle.

Lift up your heads, O ye gates, and be ye lift up, ye everlasting doors : and the King of glory shall come in.

Who is the King of glory : even the Lord of hosts, He is the King of glory.

Glory be to the Father, and to the Son : and to the Holy Ghost ;

As it was in the beginning, is now, and ever shall be : world without end. Amen.

Ant.—He shall receive the blessing of the Lord, and righteousness from the God of his salvation; this is the generation of them that seek Him.

Lord, have mercy.
Christ, have mercy.
Lord, have mercy.
Our Father.

¶ *Here let him sprinkle the body with holy water.*

℣. In my innocence hast Thou taken me;

℟. And confirmed me in Thy sight for ever.

℣. The Lord be with you;

℟. And with thy spirit.

Let us pray.

O Almighty and everlasting God, Who, although they have deserved nought, givest eternal life unto all children who are baptized and born again, as we believe Thou hast given to this one; grant, we beseech Thee, for the sake of the prayers of the Blessed Virgin Mary and all Saints, that he (she) may serve thee with a pure mind and live for ever with the blessed in Paradise. Through.

¶ *Whilst the body is taken to the grave, is said:—*

Ant.—Young men and maidens.

Laudate Dominum. Psalm cxlviii.

O praise the Lord of Heaven : praise Him in the height.

Praise Him, all ye Angels of His : praise Him, all His host.

Praise Him, Sun and Moon : praise Him, all ye Stars and Light.

Praise Him, all ye Heavens : and ye Waters that are above the Heavens.

Let them praise the Name of the Lord : for He spake the word, and they were made; He commanded, and they were created.

He hath made them fast for ever and ever : He hath given them a law which shall not be broken.

Praise the Lord upon earth : ye Dragons, and all Deeps ;
Fire and hail, snow and vapours : wind and storm,
fulfilling His Word ;
Mountains and all hills : fruitful trees and all cedars ;
Beasts and all cattle : worms and feathered fowls ;
Kings of the earth and all people : princes and all judges
of the world ;
Young men and maidens, old men and children, praise
the Name of the Lord : for His Name only is excellent,
and His praise above Heaven and earth.
He shall exalt the horn of His people ; all His Saints
shall praise Him : even the children of Israel, even the
people that serveth Him.

Cantate Domino. Psalm cxlix.

O sing unto the Lord a new song : let the congregation
of Saints praise Him.
Let Israel rejoice in Him that made him : and let the
children of Sion be joyful in their King
Let them praise His Name in the dance : let them sing
praises unto Him with tabret and harp.
For the Lord hath pleasure in His people : and helpeth
the meek-hearted.
Let the Saints be joyful with glory : let them rejoice in
their beds.
Let the praises of God be in their mouth : and a two-
edged sword in their hands.
To be avenged of the heathen : and to rebuke the
people.
To bind their kings in chains : and their nobles with
links of iron.
That they may be avenged of them, as it is written :
Such honour have all His Saints.

Laudate Dominum. Psalm cl.

O praise God in His Holiness : praise Him in the firma-
ment of His power.
Praise Him in His noble acts : praise Him according to
His excellent greatness.

E 2

Praise Him in the sound of the trumpet : praise Him upon the lute and harp.

Praise Him in the cymbals and dances : praise Him upon the strings and pipe.

Praise him upon the well-tuned cymbals : praise Him upon the loud cymbals.

Let everything that hath breath : praise the Lord.

Glory be to the Father, and to the Son : and to the Holy Ghost ;

As it was in the beginning, is now, and ever shall be : world without end.   Amen.

Ant.—Young men and maidens, old men and children, praise the Name of the Lord.

Lord, have mercy.
Christ, have mercy.
Lord, have mercy.
Our Father.

℣. Suffer little children to come unto Me,

℟. For of such is the Kingdom of Heaven.

℣. The Lord be with you ;

℟. And with thy spirit.

Let us pray.

Almighty, everlasting God, the Lover of purity, Who hast in Thy mercy taken the soul of this little one to Thy Heavenly Kingdom, have mercy upon us; and for Thy Passion's sake, and for the prayers of the Blessed Virgin Mary and all Saints, make us happy in Thy Kingdom, together with Thy Saints and elect.   Through.

¶ *Then let the Priest sprinkle the body with holy water, and cense it and the grave, after which let it be buried, and let him say returning to the Church :—*

Ant.—O all ye Elect of the Lord.

Benedicite, omnia opera.

O all ye Works of the Lord, bless ye the Lord : praise Him, and magnify Him for ever.

O ye Angels of the Lord, bless ye the Lord : praise Him, and magnify Him for ever.

O ye Heavens, bless ye the Lord : praise Him, and magnify Him for ever.

O ye Waters that be above the Firmament, bless ye the Lord : praise Him, and magnify Him for ever.

O all ye Powers of the Lord, bless ye the Lord : praise Him, and magnify Him for ever.

O ye Sun and Moon, bless ye the Lord : praise Him, and magnify Him for ever.

O ye Stars of Heaven, bless ye the Lord : praise Him, and magnify Him for ever.

O ye Showers and Dew, bless ye the Lord : praise Him, and magnify Him for ever.

O ye Winds of God, bless ye the Lord : praise Him, and magnify Him for ever.

O ye Fire and Heat, bless ye the Lord : praise Him, and magnify Him for ever.

O ye Winter and Summer, bless ye the Lord : praise Him, and magnify Him for ever.

O ye Dews and Frosts, bless ye the Lord : praise Him, and magnify Him for ever.

O ye Frost and Cold, bless ye the Lord : praise Him, and magnify Him for ever.

O ye Ice and Snow, bless ye the Lord : praise Him, and magnify Him for ever.

O ye Nights and Days, bless ye the Lord : praise Him, and magnify Him for ever.

O ye Light and Darkness, bless ye the Lord : praise Him, and magnify Him for ever.

O ye Lightnings and Clouds, bless ye the Lord : praise Him, and magnify Him for ever.

O let the Earth bless the Lord : yea, let it praise Him, and magnify Him for ever.

O ye Mountains and Hills, bless ye the Lord : praise Him, and magnify Him for ever.

O all ye Green Things upon the Earth, bless ye the Lord : praise Him, and magnify Him for ever.

O ye Wells, bless ye the Lord : praise Him, and magnify Him for ever.

O ye Seas and Floods, bless ye the Lord : praise Him, and magnify Him for ever.

O ye Whales, and all that move in the Waters, bless ye the Lord : praise Him, and magnify Him for ever.

O all ye Fowls of the Air, bless ye the Lord : praise Him, and magnify Him for ever.

O all ye Beasts and Cattle, bless ye the Lord : praise Him, and magnify Him for ever.

O ye Children of Men, bless ye the Lord : praise Him, and magnify Him for ever.

O let Israel bless the Lord : praise Him, and magnify Him for ever.

O ye Priests of the Lord, bless ye the Lord : praise Him, and magnify Him for ever.

O ye Servants of the Lord, bless ye the Lord : praise Him, and magnify Him for ever.

O ye Spirits and Souls of the Righteous, bless ye the Lord : praise Him, and magnify Him for ever.

O ye holy and humble Men of heart, bless ye the Lord : praise Him, and magnify Him for ever.

O Ananias, Azarias, and Misael, bless ye the Lord : praise Him, and magnify Him for ever.

Glory be to the Father, and to the Son : and to the Holy Ghost ;

As it was in the beginning, is now, and ever shall be : world without end. Amen.

Ant.—O all ye elect of the Lord, hasten the days of gladness, and let us give thanks unto Him.

¶ *Then let the Priest say before the Altar :—*

℣. The Lord be with you ;

℞. And with thy spirit.

Let us pray.

O everlasting God, Who hast ordained and constituted the services of Angels and men in a·wonderful order ; mercifully grant that as Thy holy Angels alway do Thee service in Heaven, so by Thy appointment they may succour and defend us on earth ; through Jesus Christ our Lord. Amen.

THE ORDER FOR

𝕮𝖍𝖊 𝕭𝖚𝖗𝖎𝖆𝖑 𝖔𝖋 𝖙𝖍𝖊 𝕯𝖊𝖆𝖉

ACCORDING TO

THE CHURCH OF ENGLAND.

THE ORDER FOR

The Burial of the Dead

ACCORDING TO

THE CHURCH OF ENGLAND.

¶ *Here is to be noted, that the Office ensuing is not to be used for any that die unbaptized, or excommunicate, or have laid violent hands upon themselves.*

¶ *The Priest and Clerks meeting the corpse at the entrance of the Churchyard, and going before it, either into the Church, or towards the Grave, shall say, or sing :—*

I am the Resurrection and the life, saith the Lord : he that believeth in Me, though he were dead, yet shall he live : and whosoever liveth and believeth in Me shall never die. *S. John* xi. 25, 26.

I know that my Redeemer liveth, and that He shall stand at the latter day upon the earth. And though after my skin worms destroy this body, yet in my flesh shall I see God : Whom I shall see for myself, and mine eyes shall behold, and not another. *Job* xix. 25, 26, 27.

We brought nothing into this world, and it is certain we can carry nothing out. The Lord gave, and the Lord hath taken away ; blessed be the Name of the Lord. I *Tim.* vi. 7 ; *Job* i. 21.

¶ *After they are come into the Church, shall be read one or both of these Psalms following :—*

Dixi, custodiam. Psalm xxxix.

I said, I will take heed to my ways : that I offend not in my tongue.

I will keep my mouth as it were with a bridle : while the ungodly is in my sight.

I held my tongue, and spake nothing : I kept silence, yea, even from good words ; but it was pain and grief to me.

My heart was hot within me, and while I was thus musing the fire kindled : and at the last I spake with my tongue.

Lord, let me know mine end, and the number of my days : that I may be certified how long I have to live.

Behold, Thou hast made my days as it were a span long : and mine age is even as nothing in respect of Thee ; and verily every man living is altogether vanity.

For man walketh in a vain shadow, and disquieteth himself in vain : he heapeth up riches, and cannot tell who shall gather them.

And now, Lord, what is my hope : truly my hope is even in Thee.

Deliver me from all mine offences : and make me not a rebuke unto the foolish.

I became dumb, and opened not my mouth : for it was Thy doing.

Take Thy plague away from me : I am even consumed by means of Thy heavy hand.

When Thou with rebukes dost chasten man for sin, Thou makest his beauty to consume away, like as it were a moth fretting a garment : every man therefore is but vanity.

Hear my prayer, O Lord, and with Thine ears consider my calling : hold not Thy peace at my tears.

For I am a stranger with Thee : and a sojourner, as all my fathers were.

O spare me a little, that I may recover my strength : before I go hence, and be no more seen.

Glory be to the Father, and to the Son : and to the Holy Ghost ;

As it was in the beginning, is now, and ever shall be : world without end. Amen.

Domine, refugium.   Psalm xc.

Lord, Thou hast been our refuge : from one generation to another.

Before the mountains were brought forth, or ever the earth and the world were made : Thou art God from everlasting, and world without end.

Thou turnest man to destruction : again Thou sayest, Come again, ye children of men.

For a thousand years in Thy sight are but as yesterday : seeing that is past as a watch in the night.

As soon as Thou scatterest them, they are even as a sleep : and fade away suddenly like the grass.

In the morning it is green, and groweth up : but in the evening it is cut down, dried up, and withered.

For we consume away in Thy displeasure : and are afraid at Thy wrathful indignation.

Thou hast set our misdeeds before Thee : and our secret sins in the light of Thy countenance.

For when Thou art angry all our days are gone : we bring our years to an end, as it were a tale that is told.

The days of our age are threescore years and ten ; and though men be so strong that they come to fourscore years : yet is their strength then but labour and sorrow ; so soon passeth it away, and we are gone.

But who regardeth the power of Thy wrath : for even thereafter as a man feareth, so is Thy displeasure.

O teach us to number our days : that we may apply our hearts unto wisdom.

Turn Thee again, O Lord, at the last : and be gracious unto Thy servants.

O satisfy us with Thy mercy, and that soon : so shall we rejoice and be glad all the days of our life.

Comfort us again now after the time that Thou hast plagued us : and for the years wherein we have suffered adversity.

Shew Thy servants Thy work : and their children Thy glory.

And the glorious Majesty of the Lord our God be upon

us : prosper Thou the work of our hands upon us, O prosper Thou our handy-work.

Glory be to the Father, and to the Son : and to the Holy Ghost ;

As it was in the beginning, is now, and ever shall be : world without end. Amen.

¶ *Then shall follow the Lesson taken out of the fifteenth Chapter of the former Epistle of Saint Paul to the Corinthians.*

I Cor. xv. 20.

Now is Christ risen from the dead, and become the first-fruits of them that slept. For since by man came death, by man came also the Resurrection of the dead. For as in Adam all die, even so in Christ shall all be made alive. But every man in his own order : Christ the first-fruits ; afterward they that are Christ's, at His coming. Then cometh the end, when He shall have delivered up the Kingdom to God, even the Father ; when He shall have put down all rule, and all authority, and power. For He must reign, till He hath put all enemies under His feet. The last enemy that shall be destroyed is death. For He hath put all things under His feet. But when He saith, all things are put under Him, it is manifest that He is excepted, which did put all things under Him. And when all things shall be subdued unto Him, then shall the Son also Himself be subject unto Him that put all things under Him, that God may be all in all. Else what shall they do which are baptized for the dead, if the dead rise not at all ? Why are they then baptized for the dead ? and why stand we in jeopardy every hour ? I protest by your rejoicing, which I have in Christ Jesus our Lord, I die daily. If after the manner of men I have fought with beasts at Ephesus, what advantageth it me, if the dead rise not ? Let us eat and drink, for to-morrow we die. Be not deceived : evil communications corrupt good manners. Awake to righteousness, and sin not ; for some have not the knowledge of God. I speak this to your shame. But some man will say, How are the dead raised up ? and with what body do they come ? Thou fool, that which thou sowest is not quickened, except it die. And that which thou sowest, thou sowest not that body that shall be, but bare grain, it may chance of wheat, or of some other grain : But God giveth it a body, as it hath pleased Him, and to every seed His own body. All flesh is not the same flesh ; but there is one kind of flesh of men, another flesh of beasts, another of fishes, and another of birds. There are also celestial bodies, and bodies terrestrial ; but the glory of the celestial is one, and the glory of the terrestrial is another. There is one glory of the sun, and another glory of the moon, and another glory of the stars ; for one star differeth from another star in glory. So also is the Resurrection of the dead : It is sown in corruption ; it is raised in incorruption : It is sown in dishonour ; it is raised in glory : It is sown in weakness ; it is raised in power : It is sown a natural body ; it is raised a spiritual body. There is a natural body, and there is a spiritual body. And so it is written, The first man Adam was made a living soul ; the last Adam was made a quickening spirit. Howbeit, that was not first which is spiritual, but that which is natural ; and afterward that which is spiritual. The first man is of the earth, earthy : the second man is the Lord from Heaven. As is the earthy, such are they that are earthy : and as is the heavenly, such are they also that are heavenly. And as we have borne the image of the earthy, we shall also bear the image of the heavenly. Now this I say, brethren, that flesh and blood cannot inherit the Kingdom of God ; neither doth corruption inherit incorruption. Behold, I shew you a mystery : We shall not all sleep, but we shall all be changed, in a moment, in the twinkling of an eye, at the last trump (for the trumpet shall sound), and the dead shall be raised incorruptible, and we shall be changed. For this corruptible must put on incorruption, and this mortal must put on immortality. So when this corruptible shall have put on incorruption, and this mortal shall have put on immortality ; then shall be brought to pass the saying that is written, Death is swallowed up in

victory. O death, where is thy sting? O grave, where
is thy victory? The sting of death is sin, and the strength
of sin is the law. But thanks be to God, which giveth us
the victory through our Lord Jesus Christ. Therefore,
my beloved brethren, be ye steadfast, unmoveable, always
abounding in the work of the Lord, forasmuch as ye
know that your labour is not in vain in the Lord.

¶ *When they come to the grave, while the corpse is made ready to be
laid into the earth, the Priest shall say, or the Priest and Clerks
shall sing :—*

Man that is born of a woman hath but a short time to
live, and is full of misery. He cometh up, and is cut down,
like a flower; he fleeth as it were a shadow, and never
continueth in one stay.

In the midst of life we are in death : of whom may we
seek for succour, but of Thee, O Lord, Who for our sins
art justly displeased?

Yet, O Lord God most holy, O Lord most mighty, O
holy and most merciful Saviour, deliver us not into the
bitter pains of eternal death.

Thou knowest, Lord, the secrets of our hearts ; shut not
Thy merciful ears to our prayer ; but spare us, Lord most
holy, O God most mighty, O holy and merciful Saviour,
thou most worthy Judge eternal, suffer us not, at our last
hour, for any pains of death, to fall from Thee.

¶ *Then, while the earth shall be cast upon the body by some standing
by, the Priest shall say :—*

Forasmuch as it hath pleased Almighty God of His great
mercy to take unto Himself the soul of our dear *brother* here
departed, we therefore commit *his* body to the ground ;
earth to earth, ashes to ashes, dust to dust ; in sure and
certain hope of the Resurrection to eternal life, through
our Lord Jesus Christ ; Who shall change our vile body,
that it may be like unto His glorious body, according to
the mighty working, whereby He is able to subdue all
things to Himself.

¶ Then shall be said or sung :—

I heard a voice from Heaven, saying unto me, Write, From henceforth blessed are the dead which die in the Lord : even so saith the Spirit ; for they rest from their labours.

¶ Then the Priest shall say :—

Lord, have mercy upon us.
Christ, have mercy upon us.
Lord, have mercy upon us.

Our Father, which art in Heaven, Hallowed be Thy Name. Thy kingdom come. Thy will be done in earth, as it is in Heaven. Give us this day our daily bread. And forgive us our trespasses, as we forgive them that trespass against us. And lead us not into temptation ; but deliver us from evil. Amen.

Priest.

Almighty God, with Whom do live the spirits of them that depart hence in the Lord, and with Whom the souls of the faithful, after they are delivered from the burden of the flesh, are in joy and felicity ; we give Thee hearty thanks, for that it hath pleased Thee to deliver this our *brother* out of the miseries of this sinful world ; beseeching Thee, that it may please Thee, of Thy gracious goodness, shortly to accomplish the number of Thine elect, and to hasten Thy kingdom ; that we, with all those that are departed in the true faith of Thy holy Name, may have our perfect consummation and bliss, both in body and soul, in Thy eternal and everlasting glory ; through Jesus Christ our Lord. Amen.

The Collect.

O Merciful God, the Father of our Lord Jesus Christ, Who is the Resurrection and the life ; in Whom whosoever believeth shall live, though he die ; and whosoever liveth, and believeth in Him, shall not die eternally ; Who also hath taught us, by His holy Apostle Saint Paul, not to be sorry, as men without hope, for them that sleep in Him ; we meekly beseech Thee, O Father, to raise us from the death of sin unto the life of righteousness; that, when we shall depart this life, we may rest in Him, as our hope is this our *brother* doth; and that, at the general Resurrection in the last day, we may be found acceptable in Thy sight; and receive that blessing which Thy well-beloved Son shall then pronounce to all that love and fear Thee, saying, Come, ye blessed children of My Father, receive the kingdom prepared for you from the beginning of the world; Grant this, we beseech Thee, O merciful Father, through Jesus Christ, our Mediator and Redeemer. Amen.

The grace of our Lord Jesus Christ, and the love of God, and the fellowship of the Holy Ghost, be with us all evermore. Amen.

Printed by the Church Printing Company, 11, Burleigh-street, Strand.